THE ANCIENT TRAVELER

Writings on Love

Swami Rama

Himalayan Institute Hospital Trust
Swami Ram Nagar, PO Jolly Grant,
Dehradun - 248016, Uttarakhand, India

With all my gratitude, exceeding love and reverence, I offer this to the Lord of my life, my Gurudeva, who brought me up in spite of my countless faults and weaknesses. Whenever I stumbled on the path, he gave me strength. To him alone I feel indebted and dedicated. I remember him with a feeling of gratitude in every breath of my life.

Swami Rama

Editing: Dr. Barbara Bova

© 2019 by the Himalayan Institute Hospital Trust
ISBN 978-81-88157-98-3
Library of Congress Control Number 2019936675

Published by:

Himalayan Institute Hospital Trust
Swami Ram Nagar, P.O. Jolly Grant,
Dehradun - 248016, Uttarakhand, India
Tel: 91-135-247-1233, Fax: 91-135-247-1122
src@hihtindia.org; www.hihtindia.org

Distributed by Lotus Press, P.O. Box 325, Twin Lakes, WI
53181 U.S.A., www.lotuspress.com, 800-824-6396,
lotuspress@lotuspress.com.

Contents

PART ONE: LOVE IN GENERAL   1
  Chapter One: What is Love?   3
  Chapter Two: Ahimsa   5
  Chapter Three: Love and Selflessness   12
  Chapter Four: Love and Nonattachment   15
  Chapter Five: Loving Your Duties   17
  Chapter Six: Love and Transformation   19
  Chapter Seven: Love as Healer   20
  Chapter Eight: Love and Nature   23

PART TWO: HUMAN LOVE   25
  Chapter One: Relationships   27
  Chapter Two: Sensual Love   34
  Chapter Three: Parental Love   41

PART THREE: SPIRITUAL LOVE   45
  Chapter One: Guru   47
  Chapter Two: My Master   49
  Chapter Three: The Divine Mother   57
  Chapter Four: Mama   60
  Chapter Five: Divine Love   68
  Chapter Six: Silence   78
  Chapter Seven: The Answer   85
  Chapter Eight: Adieu   86

PART ONE

LOVE IN GENERAL

CHAPTER ONE

WHAT IS LOVE?

Love is life.

After careful examination, I have found that a human being is on an unending journey from eternity to eternity. However, the most ancient traveler in this universe is neither man nor woman, but a mystery without which our existence would become in vain. That mystery is the very basis of life on this planet and can not be revealed by mere intellectual pursuits, psychological analysis or scientific experiments. It is unveiled only to those fortunate few who have learned to love others and thus have made love a goal of life.

I wouldn't have ordinarily thought of choosing to write on love, but since you wish to have my reflections on it, I will do so. There is a realm of love that is not accessible to intellectuals, for true lovers alone have the right to be there. In classical times when it was properly understood, love was considered a god whose divinity transcended human limits and therefore could neither be comprehended nor represented in any way. Many have made attempts before me and have taken a venture, an approach to this reality whose range of activity extends from the endless space of the heavens to the dark abysses of hell.

In my experience I have again and again been fused with the mystery of love and have never been able to explain what it is. I falter before finding a language that might adequately express the incalculable paradoxes of love. We cannot discuss one side of it without considering the other. To speak of a practical aspect is always too much or too little, for only the whole is meaningful. I involve myself in endless deception if I try to name love, showering upon it all the names and means at my command. This is a sort of confession of my imperfection and my dependence. I have come to the conclusion that one should simply cherish that love is the voice from the unknown to the known and then to the unknown again.

I feel I am a victim of cosmic love. Being only a part I cannot grasp the whole and I am at its mercy. I may ascend to it or go against it, but I am caught by it and enclosed within it. I am totally dependent upon it and am sustained by it. Love is my highlight and my darkness, whose end I cannot fathom. Love does not cease whether I speak in the tongues of men or angels or with scientific exactitude. It traces the life of the Self down to its utmost source.

God is love.

CHAPTER TWO

AHIMSA

Love bears all things and endures all things.

Nowhere will you find a true definition of love except in yoga science. In yoga science *ahimsa* means love. *A* means "no," *himsa* means "killing, hurting, harming or injuring with mind, action and speech." If you follow these rules you will be practicing love.

If you initiate the practice of ahimsa at home, the family can be a training center for learning to love others. But if you fail to love your family, you will also fail in other relationships. Husband and wife and other family members should never hurt each other. If married persons were to truly practice ahimsa, they would never quarrel. There should be an understanding in relationships that no matter what happens you will not become violent. You cannot hurt someone and at the same time say I love you.

Love is more powerful than animosity.

When animosity controls your mind, it leads your mind toward negativity. It is the defense mechanism that creates many of the problems in communication. If you are afraid of me and I am afraid of you, there can be no communication between us. Then we both become defensive and we fight. This is what happens between two nations, and that is why the whole world is fighting.

You have forgotten that we are all human beings and there is only one source that is supplying the life force to everyone, no matter which community, religion or culture one comes from. We are all the children of one Eternity, therefore you have no right to hate or harm anyone. It is not okay to love some people and hate others. If you could learn to love your enemies, they would no longer be enemies to you. Your love should travel toward expansion, not contraction. Mao Tse Dung asked, "If hundreds of varieties of flowers can grow in one garden, why can't we all flourish together in one universe?"

The practical approach to ahimsa is to practice non-violence in speech, action and thought. Gandhi, the father of the Indian nation, was completely nonviolent. He was able to get freedom from alien rule through nonviolence, without the use of guns. He exhibited the power of love to the whole of the nation and to the whole world. Somebody asked him if he believed in God, and if so what type of god did he believe in. He replied, "I believe God is truth. And to know the truth there should be truth in mind, action and speech."

Violence in speech or in action is almost always preceded by violent thoughts, which have serious repercussions on the mind and body. When you hurt someone or you think about somebody negatively, not only are you wasting time and energy, you are hurting yourself. When you hate others, it is you who suffers, not the rest of the world. All negativity can be washed away and the mind can be purified if you learn to forgive others. You also have many weaknesses and perhaps you are projecting those weaknesses onto others.

I do not understand the law that prompts mortal beings to injure each other. From where does this violence arise? What is that power that instigates people to annihilate each other's existence? I return back to my silence without any reply and with a simple conclusion that human beings have not yet really found out the art of living harmoniously. The evil that forces one to commit heinous crimes is because of *himsa,* the absence of love, consideration, kindness and awareness that we all belong to One. By killing others we are cutting the roots of the same tree whose limbs we are. This modern world is creating hell for everyone. You cannot say God is responsible for that.

Thought power is very important. Negative thoughts, emotions and violent behavior come when your reason is not functioning. Never allow your reason to retire or waste your energy on violence and negativity. Violence and anger diminish the power of love and gentleness. It is important to make effort to redirect negativity toward positive thinking. Patanjali, the codifier of yoga science, says constant contemplation on the opposite is the way to get freedom from hatred and violence. For example, if somebody hates you or if you have negative feelings toward someone, try to think of that person in a loving way.

The law is: Give and you will receive.

In the practice of ahimsa, give the best that you can selflessly to those whom you love and those who claim to love you, without any condition. If you expect something in return, then the quality of your love will be reduced by fifty per cent. Unfortunately, today the reverse is practised. You don't want to give, but you expect to receive. In the world expectation is considered to be love and is thus the mother of all problems. If you have not known the joy of doing something for others without expecting anything in return, sit down quietly and look within. Ask yourself what you have selflessly done for someone who is not related or connected to you. You will experience great joy when you do something for others without expectation.

Throughout human history and civilization there have been countless individuals who have made the pilgrimage from a narrow focus on I, me and mine to choosing to love and serve the higher good of society. And as they have increasingly dedicated themselves for the benefit of humankind and the recognition of the universal consciousness in all, numerous powers have unfolded in them for their selfless service to help others. Great individuals like Christ, Buddha, Gandhi and others all saw themselves as instruments of a higher force of consciousness, love and power in the universe, not as petty human beings preoccupied with trivial desires and pleasures. They were perfect embodiments of love and universal examples of the true expression of ahimsa.

To practise the philosophy of loving all and excluding none in daily life is to practise non-violence. There can be no hostility in the presence of one who is firmly established in the practice of non-violence. The greatest of all strengths comes from within and that is the strength of love. A gentle, loving person is very strong from within; such a person knows how to love and also how to protect himself. Self-defense is not an act of violence.

Be sensitive toward others and what they are feeling. You lose sensitivity when you become selfish and egotistical and close yourself off to others and cut yourself off from your surroundings. You remain in that shell thinking you know everything, you have everything and you are happy. When you learn to make your mind inward and one-pointed you fathom those boundaries you have created for yourself and you come to understand that deep within you is the source, the Self of all. There you will find the all-encompassing love that should emanate through your mind, action and speech. Violence is weakness. You can learn to be strong by cultivating constant awareness that you are Atman. The atman within you is the same as Paramatman.

You all aspire for love but you do not know what it is, because nobody has taught you how to love. You can know someone loves you by the way they express themselves in their speech and actions. The practice of ahimsa encompasses the principles of how to love yourself and others, and how to have that sensitivity that inspires you to serve others without expecting any reward or having any selfish motivation. Eventually, the day will come when you will start to love everyone, for beneath all these forms and names there is only one reality.

A human being needs to remain aware of the fact that he is a human being, because everyone has three natures: animal, human and divine. When you are irrational or negatively emotional, the animal aspect is predominant; you don't care what happens to anyone, and you can hurt even those whom you love. When you become a human being you like to give without expectation, and you serve others to express your love. You are human and at the same time you are God, because God is within you. Sometimes the divinity in you awakens. If you constantly remain aware of these three natures in your daily activities in life, you can become very creative. You do not have to look for God anywhere outside yourself, because God is within. Simply you have to learn how to be a human being. Through the practice of ahimsa, you can learn to love all. Then you will radiate love and your mind will remain in a state of joy. That is one of the greatest qualities you can develop. This can happen when your consciousness awakens and travels to higher dimensions.

First apply ahimsa to yourself by not hurting yourself in thought, speech or action. On the path of enlightenment one of the first things you have to learn is not to condemn yourself. You have formed the bad habit of identifying with your thought patterns, and so your thinking process controls your whole life. When you identify with your thoughts either you think you are bad or else you become puffed up with pride, neither of which is helpful. One cripples your creative intelligence and the other feeds the ego. A thought cannot make you good or bad. If a negative thought passes through your mind, it does not mean you are bad. It is your choice to accept or reject any thought that comes. The important thing is to be able to recognize which thoughts are helpful and which are to be rejected. For this you will have to sharpen the buddhi, the decisive faculty. If a thought is bad, let it be bad. It does not mean you are bad, because you are not your thoughts. You are much more than your thoughts, so there is no need to condemn yourself or feel guilty. When you become aware that the powerful, merciful Lord who is omnipresent and omniscient is within you also, you will no longer condemn yourself.

Strength lies in love not in violence.

BEAUTY

If you search for yourself to the end of the earth, you will never meet anyone like you. You are the only you and there is none to compare with you. You are exceptionally, uniquely a work of art created by the greatest of all artists, the Divine. Don't become a victim of the impositions forced upon you by this ugly society that always robs the simplicity and profundity of the beautiful. Learn to appreciate your own beauty. A human being can never hide ugliness by colorful clothes. The simpler you are, the more beautiful you look. By God, you are beautiful, and there is none equivalent to your beautiful face.

Express yourself with all the gentleness that you can, for gentleness and love are one and the same. If you learn this lesson, you can transform many lives. How beautiful is that life that knows not the ugliness of abrupt and rough behavior. The most beautiful person is one who is always filled with joy and moves in that joy. Such movements make one a great dancer. Be that and practice this dance.

CHAPTER THREE

LOVE AND SELFLESSNESS

Love means totally selfless service.

You are doing actions and you are receiving the fruits of those actions, and then again you have to do more actions. It seems there is no way of freedom. What binds you are the fruits of the actions you receive therein. The way to freedom is to give the fruits of your actions to others. If all human beings could learn to do actions for others, everyone would be free. Instead we have a society of selfish people who are expecting to attain another level of consciousness. If you really want to love someone you have to be able to sacrifice your own needs and wants. If all human efforts could be directed toward selfless service and loving the rest of humanity, love would become a constant prayer that would help everyone. Instead society is creating individuals who are like robots without the capacity to love.

According to the great sages love means to give without expectation of any award. Service done toward others is the real expression of love. Learn to love others and demonstrate that love through selfless action.

PRIME DESIRE

When heavy temptation tramples into the stillness of my living inspiration, then my little love trembles like a seed that has lost its urge for germination. Many times I have gathered the twigs of my thoughts and feelings and searched into all the corners of my heart with all my might, and many times I have been lost in the darkness. Again I have made a new altar for Thee. Verily I adore Thee as my love, the supreme benevolent and I sing the song of the Eternal.

Can I pray and ask Thee again for one of my prime desires? Tell me, what is the best way of serving humanity; what is the path that is best for all mankind? This greatest of all desires of mine is to find delight in Self-realization through serving others. I know how human beings are suffering from an age-long epidemic of ignorance and separateness. Will I see the day when all human beings will have the opportunity to observe life as a whole with its past, present and future, when everyone will attain the final goal and share all that he has with full heart and totality of mind in selfless actions? I have developed in my mind an image of truth according to an idea that I believed to be universal. One day I realized that my life had its thread of unity in the memory of the past, while ideal life dwells in the perspective of the imagination of the future. From the buried records in the dust I have realized there was something that was constantly obstructing my way. In order to remove that obstacle and give expression to my prime desire, I have gathered the facts and have come to the conclusion that my love is not imperfect but incomplete. I remain baffled and realize that some meaning of life is yet to be realized.

I am a great dreamer who wants to reveal all his personalities in the service of humanity. For several decades I have wandered in the deep valleys of the Himalayas and studied life with its currents and cross currents, and today only have I found the answer. In Thee I find my own supreme value which I call love divine. I am in bliss, at peace.

I am a wave of the Divine.

CHAPTER FOUR

LOVE AND NONATTACHMENT

Love is a source of freedom.

There is a vast difference between attachment and love. Love means to give selflessly; attachment means to possess. You repeat the word love a thousand times throughout the day without actually understanding what it is. You may say you love your boyfriend because you are attached to him, but that is not really love. Love has a sense of equality; attachment does not. Whereas love is life and knowledge, attachment has no life. In love you give selflessly and do not expect anything in return; in attachment you want to take and possess things and you have no concept of what it means to give. When you possess something, you are just expanding the domain of your ego; when you love and you are a giver, you are surrendering your ego. One who is non-attached knows the value of love. One who has known God's world can no longer remain attached to the superficial things of the world and can genuinely and unselfishly love others.

Attachment is always dependent on others or on a particular object that will inevitably change, whereas love is purely dependent on knowledge and the reality. For example, if the person whom you claim to love changes, your feelings for that person will also change. Being attached to someone may give you pleasure, but that attachment can lead you to *dvesha,* repulsion or feelings of hatred for persons or things. *Raga* and dvesha, attachment and hatred, are two sides of the same coin, thus you cannot separate them. Dvesha may cause pain when one is confronted with an object or a person one does not like or when such an aversion assumes the form of contempt, hatred or open hostility. When you become attached you become blind and forget the reality. When you are attached to certain things, they create such strong impressions in your mind that you remember those things again and again. The impressions that hatred creates are even deeper. When you hate somebody you forget all about those whom you love, because hatred is stronger than love. If you really want to understand the capacity of your love, just watch how strong your hatred is for certain persons or things. If you love somebody wholeheartedly, you can never hate that person.

Peace is not a gift that God gives to you or to anyone else. That is not His work. Although God has given you all the capacity and talents that you need, unfortunately you cripple yourself by postponing everything in the name of God. It is good to believe in God, but it is not helpful to refrain from doing your actions. No one else, not even a guru or swami, no matter how great, can give you peace. The way to attain peace is by not being attached to the things of the world and by decreasing useless desires. If you are not attached to anything and you are doing your duties skillfully, you will have peace. This requires human effort. Only those who are established in Atman, free from attachments and desires, are fully at peace. Learn to love, to grow in love and to be in love.

Love is pure and divine.

CHAPTER FIVE

LOVING YOUR DUTIES

All your actions should be prayers.

It is amazing to observe that most of the people enveloped in sloth and lethargy are not aware that life on this earth is but a brief moment, and that moment should be utilized to purify the way of the soul. Those who live in such a fool's paradise do not do their duties and yet expect the best from life. Freedom comes when you do your duties with love. You can use the duties you have assumed as a means to obtain the happiness that is the ultimate state of bliss. Whatever you do, do it with love, or don't do it at all.

A human being cannot live without doing his duties, no matter how much he tries to escape. If you do not do your duties, there is no reason for you to live in the world. However if you do your duties without love you are only a slave to your duties.

Just because they are married, wife attends husband and husband attends wife, even though they actually don't want to. They are doing duties toward each other merely as a formality. The only way to get freedom is to create love toward your duties and allow that love to grow. The question is: how to create love for your duties? You live with somebody, and after some time you get fed up and you want to change your partner. In your relationships you expect someone to love you, and that someone also expects you to love him. And so in this way love comes to mean expectation. And it is expectation that leads to misery. You are expecting so much from the world, but the world has very little to give you and so you become disappointed. This is why you go from one object to another, and you examine all the objects of the world, hoping to find something that will give you joy. Even when finally you achieve that for which you have worked your whole life, thinking it will give you joy, still you feel dissatisfied. You have not understood that no object has the power to give you joy; only your mind and heart can give you joy. Understand yourself within if you really want to be successful in the external world. Practise love by expressing love to others through selfless action.

Love means to give without any expectation.

CHAPTER SIX

LOVE AND TRANSFORMATION

Love is the greatest power on earth.

There is no need to change your house, your partner, your office, or one job for another job, because none of these will transform your personality. You may think that death has the power to change you, but death is just a habit of the body and has no power to transform human life.

One need not be a Messiah, Jesus, Buddha or Gandhi to transform consciousness on this earth. Love alone is the source of liberation and has the power to transform you. If you give love selflessly, nobody can snatch your happiness from you. Nothing can change human destiny but love. Through love you can transform the whole of society.

Transformation comes through awareness.

CHAPTER SEVEN

LOVE AS HEALER

The key to healing is selflessness.

When I was young I used to follow my master wherever he went. Once we went to a city called Heta in UP district to visit a railway officer whose only son had very severe smallpox with huge abscesses all over his body. When we were traveling it was customary to go to different households and ask for food. Being young I dashed in front of my master and knocked on the railway officer's door. When the door opened, I immediately asked, "Mother, could you give me some food?"

She came out and angrily said, "If you are really swamis, you should know that we have only one son and he is dying. Instead you are behaving like a fool and talking of food."

That really affected me. When my master reached I told him what had happened and he smiled and said, "Let me go inside."

When he saw the condition of the child he asked the mother what she had said to me. She repeated, "If you are a swami you should have known that my only son is dying. Instead of helping me you are being very selfish in asking for food."

Then again he smiled and said to me, "Son, I am going to cure him."

He then removed the bed sheet that was covering the boy and wrapped himself in that. Immediately his whole body became covered with smallpox eruptions, while the boy was completely cured. Both parents fell down at the feet of my master. He said, "Now I am going to transfer this to a tree."

Later I asked him how it was possible for him to cure that child, so he gave me one example: "Suppose there is a house that is burning, and the family members of that house are crying and screaming outside because their only child is inside that house. They have no strength to go inside and save him. Suddenly a stranger comes and hears about the child. Without hesitation he runs into the burning house and after a few moments brings the child out. How can you awaken such love where you are willing to put yourself in danger to rescue someone else? Love requires sacrifice and courage. Anyone who knows what sacrifice is and what it means to give, is a real lover."

Above and beyond medicine you can heal others if you have an intense desire to serve others with love. You have that potential, but you have not yet explored it. Human beings are still incomplete in the process of evolution. That completion will be possible when you learn to love others and serve without any selfish motivation.

The key to healing is selflessness, love, dynamic will and undivided devotion to the Lord within. Christ and all the great messengers had the capacity to heal. You also have that same capacity; you simply have to come in touch with it.

When India was ruled and controlled by the Mogul dynasty, one of the rulers, Babur, had only one son, Humayun, who was on his deathbed. So Babur went to different swamis, sages, fakirs and priests, but nobody could help that dying child. Then one of the women sages came forward and said, "You have healing powers. Why do you not heal your child?"

"But I am not a spiritual person. I am not pious and holy."

She said, "But still you have the power to heal. You can use it if you are prepared to give up your life for the sake of your son."

"Yes, I have lived for a long time, so I am willing to give up this life. If he doesn't live, I will have to go through so much sorrow in my old age."

So the lady said, "Hold this glass of water while walking around the cot four times and repeating: 'O Lord, give this span of life to my child. I quit, I surrender.' And then drink this water."

Having followed her instructions, he abruptly died. And the child was cured and got up from the bed.

Love is the real healer.

CHAPTER EIGHT

LOVE AND NATURE

My admonition and despairing cry is that most people do not care for nature and would sell their share in all her beauty for a given sum. Where are those persons who sensitively and with complete understanding love nature and its beauty? The artistic instinct is cultivated by the minds and hearts of a fortunate few. It dawns directly from the green valleys and meadows to the highest peak of sensitivity, and affords a sense of surprise and a kind of pleasing terror. In essence it is awesome, inexplicable and immeasurable. Those who are celebrants of nature remain close to the reality. The daily and hourly miracles of nature that remain unnoticed usually are enjoyed by artists and those who simply appreciate nature.

First of all they discover how new and beautiful the familiar can be when they actually see it as though they had never seen it before. To the lover of nature the wild roses and the violets are as striking as the flame tree or the bird of paradise. What is needed is the zeal to appreciate the natural world in its own setting.

The Sound of Nature

A glad day, breeze stirring
The gentle lucidity of the trees;
A smell of fragrance in the air,
The sound of nature everywhere.

Oh how calm the world could be
If only you would stop and see.

PART TWO

HUMAN LOVE

RELATIONSHIPS

Love means to adjust and to understand.

The Odd Couple

One day a sage came to visit a couple. He sang a song for them that explained the meaning of life and the true goal of life. His song expressed that love was the most ancient traveler in the world. From eternity to eternity it travels and in the course of its traveling it gives a message:

"Do as many experiments as you want, learn to love each other the way you understand, but remember that love will not last for a long time if it remains only on the physical level. Love is an uninterrupted flow of the divine and when its flow is blocked it leaves a stagnant pool. If love does not radiate through your family life, the family will also become like a stagnant pool. Love does not know selfishness. When you try to possess love, not only does it disturb you, everyone in the family suffers. You have to find love beyond the body and all the levels of mind and desires."

"But how?" asked the odd couple.

The sage said, "Have mutual understanding, mutual respect and mutual sharing; always complement each other and avoid the gulf of misunderstanding and misjudging. You can have disagreements but only for wanting to agree and not to split. Learn to talk, to behave with a feeling of giving, for giving is love. But that giving should be in a concentrated form toward only one direction and not scattered about, because it is hard to gather it again. Love can be dissipated, evaporated, exhausted and disappointed, but then talk and thrash out the differences. It's not difficult."

I was listening to this song sitting on my window sill in the guest house of the odd couple. I liked the song and have always remembered it, but I don't know if the odd couple received the message. God knows.

"Will you come back and visit us again, sir?" they asked.

The sage said, "I have sung my song, and that is my sermon. Now you should practise it. See you again."

After a few weeks this sage happened to pass the same house on his way. The odd couple had been waiting to see him to hear something new from him. They welcomed him and offered him a seat and food and water.

The sage said, "My children, I have not come with any expectation, for I don't have any. I don't have any work to do, so I have assumed this duty of visiting homes and sharing my experiences. Do you have any questions?"

The odd couple said, "Yes, sir. We have decided to separate for we are two different people who always think differently. We want to know if you have any suggestions for us."

Listening to this, the sage said, "The first mistake you have committed is that of marriage. Now, the second mistake you are about to commit is that you are going to separate. You are so young and cannot peep into the secrets of the future. Do you really know what you are up to?"

The odd couple said, "Sir, we want your advice."

"Well, as you say, you fell in love with each other and decided to get married. But when you were in love, you both presented the best of yourselves and were afraid to present your other side. Do you know, my children, that which is beautiful is also ugly, because beauty and ugliness are inseparably mingled? They are simply concepts created by the human mind for sense pleasure. Fault finding is not a joyous excursion. You should learn to accept each other, understand each other and help each other to grow. What compelled you to get married and establish a home, and what is it that has made you decide to separate and then divorce? Can you explain?"

"We were charmed by each other's faces, figures and clothes. So we thought that we were the fittest persons to fit in. Later on we found out that we both were good people, but not meant for each other."

"What is your disagreement?" asked the sage.

"We don't satisfy each others needs," they said.

"What do you mean by needs?" said the sage.

"Sir, we don't satisfy each other's sexuality," they answered.

"Is this the point of disagreement, or is there something more than this? I will give you a training program so that you can adjust, accommodate and remain sexually satisfied. But tell me my children, was it only for sexual satisfaction that you got married? If so, that was not enough reason for such a great undertaking. Why did you do this? Are you prepared to realize your mistakes and learn to live together, for there is nothing like incompatibility? This is just a word of conversation accepted by the law. If you want to be together you can be helped."

The home should radiate love. Wife and husband should learn how to be selfless with each other so they can attain the goal of life. They can create that state of joy at home by knowing the purpose of life and living life as worship.

Woman

Woman is far superior to man because of her delicate qualities, aesthetic sense and natural way of giving. Her real strength is gentleness, which has the power to turn the strongest men into mice or cowardly men into great warriors. She is a many-faceted artist whose instinctual knowledge leads her to be creative and thus she has given birth to many aspects of art such as dance, music and movement. It is woman who has established the family institution and who is the custodian of culture and family life.

Man

On the other hand, man, though he has brute force and can express himself violently, lacks the quality of sensitivity. He is not sensitive to feelings because he tends to function on the mental level rather than on feelings. Man could never go through the pain of carrying and bearing a child.

The Couple

Feeling is woman, and mind is man. Mother Nature has put them in the same cupboard, so these two separate beings, two diverse ends of the same pole, could meet and join together as a ring. Perhaps that is why the couple presents a ring to each other when they get engaged, hoping for the next step. They may think marriage is the answer to all the questions of life, but that doesn't always come true. The man full of animal passions and the woman full of giving, how enjoyable that these two strangers would decide to establish a home. The man thinks the woman is his and the woman also thinks the same of him. Some people think the institution of marriage is of no use. And you cannot blame them. Man's ideal of womanhood and woman's ideal of manliness are created by imaginative qualities according to their hopes and desires. It is a work of art to make a relationship work in a perfect way.

<u>Falling in Love</u>

Male and female are attracted toward each other because of the law of association. You may like a person on first sight, but if you never see that person again in your life, then there is nothing. However, if you continue to meet that person, love grows as you slowly try to understand each other and begin to develop consideration and respect for each other. When you are in love with someone, you are not afraid of anything. As long as you are not in love you have many fears. So better have a good lover!

When two people meet and fall in love, they become philosophers without having any philosophy. You may think you love someone and that person also loves you and will do everything for you. The other person probably also thinks the same. Even though you say you love somebody, you don't actually love them. You identify yourself with someone and say you love that person because you feel pity for them.

If you find a perpetual smile on your beloved's face, you can be sure she is in love with you. It is like the smile of a flower blossom. Don't ever pluck such a blooming flower or expect anything from your beloved, or else she might lose forever the smile she has been giving to you. The voice of a smile leaves the greatest of all imprints in the heart, which no power can ever snatch. A heart full of smiles is like a magnificent vessel of nectar.

Smiling is one virtue that is not found in any other form of creation. The capacity to smile is a gift to humans from the beloved Lord. When someone smiles, it means she has reverence for the person she is looking at. A smile shows respect for the Lord of life. Frowning and making a gloomy face and being negatively withdrawn are not creative aspects of human nature. You have become a victim of these impurities that are alien to human nature. Learn to love and smile, for smiles are the greatest of all gifts the beloved can give. A smile is a bouquet made of the flowers that grow in the garden of delight within you.

Love is a perennial smile that does not decay in any circumstances.

CHAPTER TWO

SENSUAL LOVE

Love means expansion.

You all talk about love and want to be great lovers. But you must have some object apart from yourself to love, sense and feel. This is love on the sensual level. Sex is a very powerful urge and this urge cannot be dealt with without the help of someone else. However sex is only one part of the expression of love that is based on equality. Sex is participation in an act to give comfort to each other, but life is not meant for sex alone. If you spend your whole life searching for your sexual partner, how will you do anything else in your life? If you have decided to live only for sex, then that is an entirely different thing, and you should be prepared for the consequences.

It is important to understand what sexual energy is, not only on the physical level, but especially on the mental level. Sex comes from the mind and then expresses through the body. Whereas food affects the body first and then the mind, sex affects the mind first and then the body.

And sex should not be reduced to a habit. If it becomes a habit then you will have to curtail all your other activities and think of sex alone. When that happens, sex becomes a very dangerous drive and can create many illnesses. To discipline means to follow nature. But if you are not natural and you are doing something out of habit, that habit will predominate and run your life so that you will have no control over yourself. If there is no control over the sexual faculty, you will have to learn to sublimate that urge. If you do not know what sublimation is or how to control the sexual urge, it is better that you should have only one sexual partner. That is better for mental health also because excessive sex can make you mentally sick. If you go on doing sex with anybody you meet on the way, you will find that you have become sick, because uncontrolled sex affects the mind. Actually love should be developed slowly and gradually. Self control can lead you to that, but that has to be cultivated.

Very few people are educated where sex is concerned and so they don't get satisfaction in the sexual act. When man is not satisfied, he runs here and there. One who is not satisfied cannot satisfy another. Man cannot satisfy woman because he hasn't tried to understand her. He is selfish from the very beginning and as far as biological necessity is concerned, man wants to fulfill his animal desires and to be free. He is irresponsible and does not want any bondage in life. There are men who are never satisfied with one woman, no matter who she is. Man by nature is a polygamist, woman is not. It is man who is not sincere to his wife. Woman likes to live with one man, whereas man likes to run around. Woman can be led to do so out of frustration and she can become the greatest bitch, no doubt. And then there is no limit. She can become treacherous. I heard someone say his life was empty and he didn't feel content with the woman with whom he was living, therefore he got married again. I spontaneously said, "A man loving and living with two women does injustice to all three."

Hearing my words, he became pensive and wanted to know why I had said such a thing. I replied that in the path of love there is no possibility for two to walk together, for the lane of love is too narrow for two to pass through it. Two hearts having one soul complement one eternal love. For walking on the path of love two have to become one and one alone. Therefore, my dear friend, having two objects of love is a sheer distraction, and that is the reason you are miserable. You are a victim of your loves. Have you done justice to yourself and to those two innocent women? A man loving two women at the same time does injustice to all three. Laying his hand on his mouth, he was baffled and bewildered and started to cry. I told him that which has been done could not be undone. Certain mistakes once committed could never be rectified. Therefore, they should be intellectually and philosophically dismissed with the promise not to be repeated again. God help you. I don't have any remedy for you.

I have seen sexual disparity everywhere because people are not trained to understand both energies, male and female. Man does sex to satisfy his ego, to show off that he is a man. Sometimes the man is in a different mood due to economical and financial pressures so he becomes very hasty in the sexual act. He wants to relieve his tensions and emotions and calls it love. When you make love it should never be emotional. If you are emotional, it will be disastrous for your health, especially your mental health. Emotions should be under your control. If that emotion which is related to your sexual life is not properly directed, it will definitely lead to frustration. You have to understand each other's behavior and thoughts and accept each other as you are.

If the sexual act is not comfortable it means there is no understanding, and without understanding there can be no love. Sex without love is animal in nature, and is no different than masturbation. Love that is related to sense objects and sensual pleasures is actually lust, not love. Masturbation and sexual union are two different things. Masturbation is biological compulsion; the desire for sexual union comes from the urge to go beyond, to unite yourself with the absolute truth.

Both should be prepared for the sexual act. What happens is that when the man is active, the woman remains in a calm and passive mood. And when there is arousal in the woman, by that time the man has become passive. This complaint frequently comes up in sexual partners and is a problem everywhere. Compatibility comes when the partners have adjusted to each other and know each other.

If two people are to live together they have to share their minds and thinking. You have to understand your partner's mind before you can enjoy his or her body. Many times I have heard a married couple say they have lived together for 40 years and shared the same bed, but they have never known each other. This is because they haven't shared their thinking. If you have not learned to share your thinking, your mind and your whole being, you cannot love someone. Even if you get the best of partners, but you are not happy or if your mind is somewhere else and you are not mentally attracted to your partner, you both will not enjoy the sexual act. Sharing the body is not sufficient for love. If after forty years you finally realize you have never known each other, why have you lived together for forty years? People tend to stay married because they cannot live without having each other to lean on. That is love in the world. This type of love is not fulfilling or complete and can create a serious barrier to enlightenment. Many couples pretend to be happy because they expect that happiness will eventually come.

Expectation is the cause of many marital problems. You expect too much from your partner, even though that person may not have the capacity to fulfill your expectations. Man expects his wife to love him, to look after him, to serve him and to do what he says. She should fulfill all his sexual desires and behave as he wants her to. Wife also thinks similarly and expects her husband to love her and to listen to her. This results in a clash between the two wants and two expectations because you are both just expecting, without giving. You expect so much from each other, and call it love. That is why you are miserable. If you cannot adjust in sexual understanding, both will be dissatisfied, and the marriage will fall apart. It is better to try to understand each other well, and to be prepared for all the difficulties and obstacles before getting married.

Spirituality and Marriage

Two people get along when they think in a similar way, act in a similar way, and feel in a similar way. Wife and husband can live together without having any problem if they both are spiritual people. It is spirituality that brings husband and wife together; nothing worldly can bring them together. Worldly ties are not stable and can never make you secure. You should definitely have worldly goals, but more importantly you should have a purpose of life and both should work for that purpose. Then you can lead a sexual life and at the same time live happily and divert your resources toward the goal of enlightenment. That is possible in this very life.

When you and your partner are both really giving and loving, then that giving becomes a great joy. If you learn to give from the very beginning, then sex will be very enjoyable. Giving love itself is rewarding. But if you both want to take, then who will give? When you both learn to give, then those two energies will create a flame, the flame of love. That spark is a spark divine. As long as the fire of love is alive, love remains fresh and new. But when it diminishes, love disappears.

In the sexual act it is not the object that is the source of pleasure; it is the life force that is to be enjoyed. That energy should move upwards. When you have completely given everything and you have become lost in that giving, that unity leads you to a state of joy, *vishayananda*, a momentary experience of the joy of eternity. That is why you keep trying to fulfill that urge completely, but it can never be fulfilled. You spend your whole life in repeating that and trying to expand that moment. It's like a thirst that is never quenched. No ocean in the world has the power to quench that thirst.

Life has two laws, the law of expansion and the law of contraction. And you are not satisfied so you want to continue it and go beyond that. That spark, that moment leads you toward expansion. Love means expansion. But when you are selfish you contract and withdraw yourself, instead of giving and expanding. You also have to know when to give and when not to give. Sometimes you become very frustrated. Then you can damage yourself and your emotional body if you go on giving out of the way to the place where you have not to give. And sometimes it can damage you where you have to give and you cannot give. It happens.

So let your needs be healthy so that you attain your goal. Let you not disturb yourself in the name of love and joy. Learn to understand and serve each other; help each other, love each other and share with each other. Those who want to realize the greatest delight should realize themselves in others. This is the definition of true love. This love offers testimony of the whole, which is the final truth to be attained. The spirit of love is boundless and emancipates our being from illusory bonds and superimpositions. It is unity that will lead us to truth. That which is the beginning and end of the phenomenal world is divine.

Love is the highest of commitments.

CHAPTER THREE

PARENTAL LOVE

The best method of communication is through the heart.

When children are given care and love, they will spontaneously return that love. Newborn babies silently communicate with their mother through the language of love, the most ancient of languages and the mother of all languages.

It is love that a child needs most, and that love should be completely selfless, not based on the idea that the child is your possession. You should love your child because you recognize that your child is a human being who has the capacity to do many things in life and to become someone great in the world.

The most ancient traveler in the world is human love. When a child is born, he first loves his mother's bosom. Slowly that love moves toward toys and sandcastles that the child builds. As the child grows, it moves to girlfriends or boyfriends. Later, love shifts to degrees and honors from universities, after which it grows for prestige, position and the desire to own something to satisfy the ego. That love grows again for a woman or a man, for marriage and for a home and children. Finally, one wants to find out what love really means. Sometimes those who have lived life very sincerely sit down and laugh. "Honey, what is that love? We are satisfied with our relationship but we have not really known what love means." This indicates that although you may have done your duties as a good spouse and parent, you have not yet learned to really love. That is why you are still not satisfied and you feel that you have to gain something. What is missing is an understanding of the purpose of life. The ancients used to teach their children everyday before going to bed, "I am strong; I am not afraid of anything, because I love all and exclude none. The purpose of my life is to serve others, to help others and to love others." If children today were to grow up in such an environment, they could become great people who would serve society and stand as examples for others.

You do not know what love is, even though you use this word in daily life. A child can teach you what love is. In the early years children are selfish. Their love is self-love, and for that they love their parents. Slowly that love expands, and they start to have consideration for their parents, friends and environment. But from the very beginning they are self-centered, and if they are not trained to give, this deep-rooted attitude will remain with them their whole life.

If a child has not been properly cared for by either parent at all the critical stages of development, when the child grows up he or she will project those unmet needs onto his or her spouse. For such a person, the husband or wife becomes the father or mother respectively. This leads to lifelong incompatibility. The home is meant for you and your family to learn how to love.

A Sanskrit verse says you should love your children unconditionally up to the age of five. After the age of five children need both love and discipline. When you love them, love them without any reservation. And sacrifice your pleasures for the sake of that love.

A child is a great joy and can teach you the greatest lesson in life. Only those who have children can know how much God loves them. The way you love your child, the way you protect your child and sacrifice for your child, so God also loves you, because you are His child.

The actual foundation of the process of human growth is love.

PART THREE

SPIRITUAL LOVE

GURU

Guru lives in the world but does not belong to the world.

The guru wants nothing for what he is doing because it is his duty and the purpose of his life. If he guides you, he is not obliging you; he is merely doing his work. He cannot live without doing his duty selflessly, for selfless love is the very basis of enlightenment. Such gurus guide humanity and radiate life and light from the unknown corners of the world. The world is not aware of them, and they do not want recognition. You may try your best to do something for your guru, but you cannot, because he doesn't need anything. As the sun shines and lives far above, the guru gives spiritual love and remains unattached. This is why you should give your love and respect to your guru. If my guru and the Lord were to both come to me, I would go to my guru first and say, "Thank you very much. You have introduced me to the Lord." I would not go to the Lord and say, "Thank you very much, Lord. You have given me my guru."

In addition the guru should have inner strength and compassion. Compassion means that the teacher loves his students and wants them to grow and practise. If compassion is not there, then imparting knowledge is like planting seeds in a barren field in which nothing will grow.

You can feel if someone is phony or genuine when they say they love you. What do you mean by the word love? Love is when someone does things for you and does not expect anything in return. But if a teacher expects money or something else from his students, then that is a labor fee and has nothing to do with teaching. If you ask, "Guruji how much do you love me?" The teacher will reply, "My dear chela, as much as you love me, I love you the same."

I spent the first forty years of my life going to many teachers. It became like a hobby to me. In vain I was roaming here and there, journeying far and wide, crossing the mountains and seven seas to seek and discover myself. Then finally I realized the teacher is within me. All I could do was laugh at myself and my foolishness. People called me wise, whereas I should have been called stupid for searching for myself outside instead of being still and looking within to become aware of what I already am. Finally I realized that I was the most extravagant vagabond I had ever met for wasting my breath and time searching for myself here, there and everywhere.

I am not condemning teachers, because they help. But if you ignore the teacher within, you will not be able to open the keys of the book of life. Your conscience is the greatest guide within you, but you do not listen to it because you don't have self-confidence. Once you deserve to tread the inner path, everything will be open for you. And don't worry about the mistakes; you are bound to commit mistakes when you are learning. In the process of learning, mistakes become the pillars of success, provided you don't give up.

CHAPTER TWO

MY MASTER

Sage of the mountain.

He was a great soul of an incomparably great nature who positively touched the infinite. An illumined presence, he was an echo from the depths of being, fully bathed in the light of fire. As he walked, anyone who saw him felt the rhythm of his cosmic union with the unseen and wondered about the mysteries of the king of Silence.

His wisdom was as old as the Himalayas and younger than childhood; his philosophy belonged to no school. His love for his disciples was the song of songs. He knew neither hope nor fear but dwelled in the calm of the spiritual universe, which nothing but the human heart could comprehend.

Real Master

I went with him for the love of God,
Though the way was long for his mountain abode.
Real master, so brightly clad,
I saw no other like that;
His moonlit hair fell long,
gleaming like winter snow.

He did not speak, as he was in the Silence.
But still he lifted his head
and gazed at me with a gentle smile.

Suddenly I heard his voice,
louder than a thundering cloud.
Real master. I heard the heavy sun,
But could not see if it was in the sky or on the ground.
Hoping to find the answer,
I turned my head around.

At first he was lying on the shore across the ocean,
then standing on the mountain across the shore,
using the earth as a bridge.

Beneath the tides of day and night
with flame and darkness ridge,
I raised myself from my knee
And went to the Silence hostel.

Beloved,
Supreme teacher,
All questions disappear into thy Silence.

At Thy Holy Feet

Child am I of a sage of the mountain,
Free spirit am I, light walks by my side.
Fearless live I above glacial fountain,
In the seclusion of Himalayan cavern reside,

With snowy weather beating around me,
Ascending the peaks of the mountains I go.
No one talks with me, no one walks with me,
As I cross streams and tramp glacial snow.

I roam in the mountains that hark to the skies
And of silence have made me a friend.
My love whispers to me with silent replies
And guided by thee I ascend.

These days dwell I in a foreign land,
Missing the Ganga and silvery sand.
Holding within my sacred bosom,
Thy blessing, grace and ancient wisdom,

Offering my life at thy holy feet,
Loving all—selfless and complete.*

*Reprinted from *Love Whispers* by Swami Rama, a Himalayan International Institute publication, (c) 1986.

Guru Purnima

O Beloved Guru
Thou who art my very self
As the full moon reflects the sun's light
This body should reflect thy glory,
Thy light should shine out from every pore
And thy fire should burn away any obstruction.

Thy will be done.

<u>My Gurudev</u>

Thy memory has made a permanent abode
in the inner chamber of my being.
Thy words are like the pouring of a clear spring of
pure water onto the parched areas of my life.

From the far horizons of the world beyond
often comes a calm voice,
to remind me that the inner spirit
is the sole reality,
and that the fulfillment of this spirit
is the secret of life.

In This Hall of Thine

Somehow on this autumn Sunday
with the sunlight that shifted between
the tall deodor trees,
the rustle of dead leaves
began to drift across my memory.

It seemed appropriate to imagine
I knew my master more
when he did not mutter a word,
surrounded with silence.

I could hear
the voice of his thoughts,
singing to himself
his own songs.

Something
of the outer shell
we may come to know,
but the whole person
never.

The Last Moment

On the eve of parting day his kingliness of pose was an expression of nothing but tenderness. The serenity of northern winter was smiling on his face, something of the austere calm of snowy ranges. But his set eyes were, as ever, compellingly alive.

Whatever is finished in the realm of matter soon goes to death. It is the eternal quest for perfection that gives meaning to life and integrates all our varied activities. It was his own desire that lead him to cast off his mortal frame.

There was a stir as a sudden expectation filled the room. His gray hair stood out around his head as if charged with electricity. The perennial smile on his mouth turned into silence. The heavy lidded eyes had often held a quizzical look, but now it was over.

We had both traveled by different roads, surely the end was one. The intangible bond linking us was the bond of personal surrender to the timeless and eternal.

Now remains the leave alone.

To Him Who is the Lord of My Life

On the hour of parting
I have nothing to offer you
but a token of my deep reverential affection
and gratitude.

I who cannot give anything to you,
ramble into the garden of my mind
and the eternal valley of my spirit
to gather the fairest flowers I can find.

As my thoughts dwell lovingly
on your holy feet,
I am lifted to a higher level
of effort and devotion.

When I contemplate on the meaning of life,
I remember you saying the day would come
when your love for humanity would deepen the
      furrows
from which should spring a richer harvest of
      inspiration.

In the sweet solitude of those moments,
your voice echoes
and I start to cry.

CHAPTER THREE

THE DIVINE MOTHER

Lady of my dreams.

When I studied the Bhagavad Gita once, twice, thrice and many times, I found out it was She who was my real mother, who gave me freedom from the sadness and sorrow that I had always received from the so-called joys of the world. There was nothing that had not been given to me—the best of things: objects, friends, and above all the best of all countries, Bharata, which means love for knowledge. But all my distress and sorrow vanished only after studying the Gita. I used to sit for hours and hours, days and days, months and months, and years and years in the blessed bosom of the Bhagavad Gita, my Mother Divine. I found out that nonattachment is actually the pure divine love that bestowed on me fearlessness, happiness and joy. And that is how I live.

My love for You is immense and enormous, unmeasured by any logical standards. It is free without any expectation. I know with certainty that You are always seated in the inner chamber of my being, though Your sense of dignity does not allow You to express Yourself. Your personality persistently intrigues me and I have made up my mind to go into it more thoroughly. I am completely fascinated and have buried myself in this thought that I hold in my heart. I am not trying to solve the riddle of an unknown vision. I already know that You are the same lady of my dreams. At present my whole being is permeated and held together by one idea and goal: namely to penetrate into the secrets of my object of love.

I am lonely, but that loneliness has not been created by the absence of people around me. It has been created by my own self, for I feel I am closer to my love of loves and, therefore, I am a superior being and no one can communicate with me. I have been repeatedly warning You that my love is like an ancient traveler who will not stop unless it annihilates Thy beauty forever and ever. Now, do You know what love is? It is that something which I do not want to share with anyone but You alone.

Nightflash

To my enormous astonishment She was completely unchanged. She spoke and acted as if nothing had happened in the meanwhile. At the time I was greatly surprised and overwhelmed by what was taking place. It was as though two rivers had united and in one grand torrent were bearing me inexorably toward one goal. This experience intoxicated and overwhelmed me as it rocked me on the waves of an infinite ocean. It was an enchanting and rewarding experience that I could never forget.

You have access to all the worlds, fountainhead of my love. You have awakened me from my sacred dreams. I was dreaming the dream of eternal royalty, of its divine nature, and of union with its unfettered universality. It is that of the free man, the true freedom of birth into self-existent divinity. Whatever I do and however I live, my free soul lives in the Divine.

I am That.

CHAPTER FOUR

MAMA

In later years Swamiji wrote a loving letter to Mama (Ann Aylward) from his ashram in Nepal. It is exemplary of his unconditional love for Mama, who helped to establish the Himalayan International Institute of Yoga Science and Philosophy in America and served as its first Chairperson. Swamiji's relationship with Mama was a living illustration of the eternal bond of love that travels uninterruptedly throughout centuries and millennia, across the borders of endless lifetimes, and remains ever true. In general this letter provides insight into Swamiji's deep personal thoughts and feelings, and his general perspective on love. It is a priceless example of his poetic expression.

Beloved Mother,

I am sorry that I could not write you earlier but I am lucky to have a mother like you. I have luck and it is this that has protected me thus far in a land where no one knew me. It is as if a great pilot has been steering my ship through innumerable rocks. The major decisions of my life have been taken under a sort of plan, and yet when the choice is made I have a feeling that an invisible hand has been guiding me for purposes other than my own. The little success I have made is because of your loving grace. My mistakes are in large part due to my own folly, but grace is because of you.

Yes, I have met my aunt and did not speak a rash or a profane word of anything that my soul has held as a secret. This attitude of respect for her is there in my marrow and bones, but I can never love her.

The challenge of the people of my family and critics has impelled me to find out what is living and what is dead, and I am fully aware of it. My Rani Ma, feelings for me are not rational but love must express itself in a reasonable thought and fruitful action. The weakness of my blind faith has drawn me into disgrace and is today blocking my way, because the people with whom I live are confused between tradition and truth. I will preserve the spirit of truth which will guide me into all truth. Truth is greater than the greatest of all teachers.

I see things happening in this civilized world today that recall the worst phases of the dark ages. People have lost their conscience and have set up new gods in place of God who has been dethroned. Mother, love is an expression of the spirit first, and then mind and body. Achievements of knowledge and power are not enough. The expression of love is very essential. I had no opportunity to express myself because you did not allow me to do so.

I think God is the great silent sea of infinity with love and mercy and I leave myself at His mercy. Again I feel I have been lucky of having His and your grace. I always say he to whom life has been kind should not accept this fortune as a matter of course. It is His grace and thy grace too.

You know my life had been a constant series of accidents, surrounded by miserable surroundings and subjected to tragic blows. I have not forgotten those days of childhood when all the privileges given to me by God were denied by human beings. Now I know that no one can give me anything nor take away anything from me.

A friend of mine who has known me since my childhood made a comment rather sarcastically that I am incapable of indignation, that I am foolproof and suffer gladly. His observation is not untrue. I have ideas of my own which may be theoretically divided into good or bad, but I love them. The world has queer notions about things happening around it. People use good and bad words for their own convenience.

I am glad and happy that I have been brought by God into your contact and I do not think it is a chance or coincidence. Desire works unseen through the force of nature. Mom, apparently unimportant happenings sometimes play an important part in our lives. There is such a thing called gravitation of love. We cannot wholly tell as to why certain people attract us. We cannot help responding to them and find them interesting. Beauty can never understand itself. Attraction can only partly be explained by the poets. The real cause of our likes and dislikes are usually hidden deep down in the obscure recesses of our nature. They have little to do with our reason and logic and we cannot account for them. Wonderful have been a few experiences in this life—some are sweet and some are sour. Through them I have known the real values of life with its currents and crosscurrents. I think a richer and fuller life is open for me. These experiences have forged links of human affection and regard, have given me high joys as well as deep sorrows and have become inextricably interwoven with the fabric of my life. These experiences in a sense have made for genuine fulfillment of my destiny.

I have had my share of anxiety, trouble and sorrow, but I have had blessings too—more than I deserve—the chief being affection and kindness which I have received in abundance from you. Yes, Mom, everyone's life has two sides: one is the ordinary life we show the public and the other we carry secretly in our hearts. We want to live one imaginary life in other people's ideas of us and then we direct our efforts to seeing what we are not. My strength is being invaded and the procession of thoughts has led me to the silence within. Life is like a mysterious fabric woven of chance, fate and character, but I blame fate alone. Today again I am vacillating about the choices I have made.

My Mom is great. She is like a flower blooming with all its beauty, intelligence and glamour! I know I have to complete a few tasks and responsibilities with scientists living in that profoundly meaningful place, but this might bring a new chance to the very task that I have been doing.

Here in Nepal tradition takes the place of instinct. People feel that they are born for their traditions. In regard to them, there is a certain degree of inadaptability. Those who live in the East are not free to choose for themselves. Insofar as a person lives according to tradition and obeys it intuitively, he leads a life of faith, of belief. The need for reality arises when faith and tradition are shaken. In this part of the world the parents think for grownup children so no one gets a chance to grow. They have no life of their own. Americans are fortunate because they do not live within the boundaries of dead tradition. However Americans are troubled with vain memories and useless quarrels. But overall they are the best people in the world. Here people live with tradition and prejudices. I feel that non-dogmatic apprehensions will provide the essential means to establish a real life, but is it possible for a society like this to establish such a society as that? I think it will take several hundred years for them to do so. Confucius said: "He who by remembering the old can gain knowledge of the new is fit to be a real man." I know it is a prodigious task for me to insert something into the minds of this nation for this nation has built boundaries around itself for centuries together, and to break through these boundaries seems to be a hard task.

I have been busy in public lectures. I have undertaken all these responsibilities very carefully and comprehensively. Success seems to be easy here. I make people aware and help them understand the facts of life. I don't want to be Jourdainian, like he who had been speaking prose all his life without knowing it.

I want to tickle your vanity and tell you that you are simply beautiful. Mom, sufferings are for me and their pathology is for my master and you. I decline to write frankly about my departure for the States for everything is uncertain so far. The other day your voice was delightful and a source of consolation. I assure you I do not suffer from the mode of detachment. I know how to love and your loving words have amazed me. I am grateful for the grace of your language that is free from a display of words.

The East is full of contrasts and every genius or creative person is subject to carping criticism. I love this part of the world but no one realizes how great is the mental strain that my stay in Nepal and India imposes on me. It is a moral loneliness that is a constant and invisible burden that oppresses me most. I am lonely for your love. You promised me and I accepted it with great delight. You inspire me to compose my inspirations. In a way I calmly enjoy all situations. My religion is not a reconciliation of the diverse tides rising from the bottom of the ocean of my heart. So often I say that love, service, humanity, beauty and laughter are my real companions.

Now, you wanted to know what I do the whole day. Sometimes I go to see places of interest or endeavor to acquire inward peace; sometimes I listen to the rush of winds and torrents and the music of birds and leaves. Then I return home with freshness in the spirit. I often feel lonely and miss you a lot. Let me tell you again that love does not depend on human effort. I wish I could jump out of myself and prove my worth to you. Don't be afraid. I do not lean on anyone for any support. The lamp of love burning inside is my real support. My love is experimental and provisional in its nature. That stimulates my mind and does not hurt others. My love is not a figment of my mind; it is a real symbol of the absolute reality—a phenomenon well founded here and now. I find the future full of promise. It is a mystery to me to understand that personal love could be a social utility. So far I have been giving the benefit of the doubt to my friends and now I feel sick of my crazy dreams. No more friends, students and acquaintances. I am happy unto myself. My learning about friendship proved useless and my quest meaningless.

Verily I get the same vision of the two triangles placed upside down signifying the penetration of the lower and higher person. Whenever my thoughts lead me to darkness a new light is revealed. Many times I have heard the voice of silence saying that as long as you are dominated by your passions and desires there will be no peace. Love is not mere contemplation of the truth but suffering for it. Suffering is not punishment but a reward and a gift of love, and the reward is received when you are no more there. Love for humanity has been taught by all great people. But the capacity to love is hard to attain.

Again I will make an attempt to draw a few thought sketches tomorrow. Till then, good night. See you soon.

Yours in the service of the Lord,
Swami Rama

What do I do?

I pick up the blossoms dropped by night,
I listen to the whispers of the silence,
I contemplate on the vast void within,
I babble Her name in each breath of my life,
I revere the beauty of Her radiant face.
When the sun comes out of bed I retire.
I enter the depths of void
And breathe in the eternal fire.
Through the clouds of joy,
The wingless bird of my spirit soars higher and higher.
I am in love and fused beyond desire.

And that's what I do.*

*Reprinted from *Love Whispers,* by Swami Rama, a Himalayan International Institute publication, (c) 1986.

CHAPTER FIVE

DIVINE LOVE

Love for God means love for all.

Human love is not perfect. But if you do not have a major transfusion of human compassion, you can never have divine love. Only when you learn to truly love will you understand that love is the Lord of life.

No matter how much sadhana you do, first you have to understand the law of equality of love: the sun shines for all, the moon pales its light for all and the breeze blows for all equally. There is no disparity except when the individual self declares: "This is mine, this is mine; this is not mine."

In ancient days there were people who could see the face of God. Someone once asked me why people could not see His face anymore. I replied that one must stoop a little to fetch water from the stream; nowadays no one can stoop so low.

Many prophets have come to this earth. The prophets of today can become builders of heaven, music makers or dreamers of discourse, but without love all hopes will finally crumble to dust. Many times they have tried to establish their world over the world created by God and have called it religion. Where are they today? In their shattered state of madness they have quit this world. This is why I call them quitters and not prophets of love. They have merely tangled humanity into various knots. One prophet professes something, another teaches knowledge, still another teaches yoga. They teach this and that philosophy, but only the prophet of love can help to transform the sufferings of humanity. The world is suffering because no one knows what love is, although we all have the same capacity to understand the true meaning of life.

Love for a human being is different than love for God. Love for God means love for all. There is one life force in all human beings, animals and even plants. This is life itself. But you have no time to love life itself because you are too busy loving those things you think are essential for life. Loving things of the world first, without knowing the reality beneath all these different forms and names, is not going to help the human race. The day you are awakened to the highest knowledge you will really start to love. Once you become aware of love itself, that which is eternal and not subject to change, death and decay, you will be able to love all things.

Love for life, love without an object, is the highest of all loves.

We all are like small light bulbs. When a bulb is broken, nothing happens to the electricity. Similarly nothing happens to the life force when we disappear from this earth. You do not want to accept this because you do not want to understand the whole process. Birth is mingled with death; they are one and the same thing. You should accept this fact and live here and now. Enjoy every bit, every moment and every part of life. Your past experiences and future imaginations distract you and have caused you to forget the whole purpose of life. You have forgotten that life is something eternal and you are part of eternity. No matter which culture, religion, or philosophical background you come from, you all have one and the same purpose of life, and that is to attain perennial happiness, everlasting bliss and peace. When the love of the world is changed from a sense experience to a soul experience, it will be founded on the love of God.

There is something beyond religions. Religion is an act that is humanity's relationship with God. It is essential in the preliminary stage but surely does not allow one to be one with the whole. It is like being a moth that eats Kashmir wool trying to prove to other moths that Kashmir exists. God's existence in reality does not depend on our proofs. There is something wrong with the philosophers and theologians for they have the curious notion that God is a kind of hypothesis that could be analyzed and discussed. God to me is a real annihilating fire and indescribable grace. I accept both. Everywhere in the realm of religion I have encountered locked doors. If ever one door should chance to open, I was disappointed by what lay behind it.

My religion knows neither hope nor fear. It dwells in the calm of the spiritual universe, which nothing but the human heart can comprehend. When the dew drop in the grass mirrors the heavens, why can't the human mind and heart?

When one's whole being is saturated with the idea of love from head to foot, then every pore of the body becomes alive to cosmic consciousness.

Your outer individual shell will remain exactly the same, but your inner light will expand to universal consciousness. That individual flame of love will become a forest conflagration and will burn up the precarious weed of selfishness. In love, you want to give and feel great joy in giving. Truth will automatically come to you if you learn how to love selflessly. The language of love comes from the soul through the heart.

The highest of all religions and all practices is love.

Golden Light

Golden light came down into my heart
and my life was smitten with Thy eternity.

Now has it manifest a temple where Thou art,
and all its passions point toward One.

Potent Indweller,
Thou dost breathe this body
and fill it with Thyself.

Music and thunder and the cries of birds,
Life's babble of her sorrows and joys,
the cadence of human speech
and murmured words;

All voices have become Thy voice.

Flight of My Immortal Will

I have become foam, a white sea of bliss,
I am a curling wave of the Lord's delight,
a shapeless flow of happy passionate light,
a whirlpool of the streams of paradise.

My pinions soar beyond time and space
into unfairy light;
I bring the bliss of the Eternal's face
and the boon of the spirit's sight.

Nothing is hidden from my burning heart,
my mind is soarless and still;
my song is shoreless and mystic art,
my flight immortal will.

I have become foam, a white sea of bliss,
I am a curling wave of the Lord's delight,
a shapeless flow of happy passionate light,
a whirlpool of the streams of paradise.

And So We Meet

Energy purge,
The moment stops,
All else forgotten.
And so we meet.

Thy laughter vibrates
throughout this body.
Mantra repeating itself.
Pleasure so great,
The ego loses control and fears.

Forbear this fear.
Grace abounds,
teaching that we are love,
Showing us our reality.

O Love—
Inhale this fire
And feed it with Thy prana.

Soham, hamsa.

The Lotus of My Love

Lo! A glitter of light,
the purple gleaming at the apex of the Himalayas,
who doubts that it shall finally pervade the planes of
    the Ganges?
Quickened by the first touch of the rising sun,
the lotus of my love opens its petals,
harboring the life of heaven in its luster and scent.

The Living Truth

I have gathered my dreams in my inner chamber
    Between the sun and the moon.
And preserved them softly and kept them there,
    My precious dreams of You.

I have been digging deep and long
    Mid a horror of filth and mire
A bed for the golden river's song
    A home for the deathless fire.

I have suffered and labored day and night
    To bring the fire to man;
But the hate of hell and human spite
    Are my mead since the world began.

For man's mind is the dupe of his animal self;
    Hoping its lust to win,
He harbors with him a grisly elf
    Enamored of sorrow and sin.

All around is darkness and strife;
    For the lamps that men call suns
Halfway gleam on this stumbling life
    cast by the undying ones.

Man lights his torches of hope
    That lead to a failing edge,
A fragment of truth is his widest scope,
    An inn his pilgrimage.

The truth of truths men fear and deny,
    The light of lights they refuge;
To ignorant gods they lift their cry
    or a demon altar choose.

My gaping words are a thousand and one.
    But I cannot rest till my task is done
How they mock and sneer, both devils and men!
    Painting the sky with its fiery stain.

A voice cried "God!" where none have gone.
    Dig deeper and deeper yet
Till thou reach the firm foundation stone
    And knock at the keyless gate.

A little more and the new life's doors
    Carved in silver light,
With its aureole roof and mosaic floors
    in a great world bare and bright.

I shall leave my dreams in their argent air.
    For in a raiment of gold and blue
There shall move on the earth embodied and fair
    The living truth—of You.

CHAPTER SIX

SILENCE

Silence gives us ultimate peace, happiness and bliss.

All of wisdom flows from one source, the center of silence. And to attain that silence, we find in all great traditions some sort of prayer, word, mantra or sound that leads us to the silence. Modern man doesn't understand that silence and doesn't know how to be in silence. Fake prayers, fake promises and fake words will not help you. You have spoken so much, written so much and heard so much, now you should learn something about silence.

There are three streams through which wisdom flows: firm faith in the highest self, the teachings that are filtered through a pure heart and mind and the voice of a clear conscience. When a decision is difficult or impossible, then go into the mountain in solitude, or into the retreat of your soul or weigh the word of Providence. Accept not hastily all voices for they may be waiting to rob your faith. Let your heart be pure and your mind intent and then follow the way of Providence. All wise thoughts and words proceed from the silence of infinity. He who would attain divinity must endure endless trials, but most seekers are eager instead to offer bribes. As the bee suckles the nectar of the flowers, so the seeker gathers twigs for the sacred fire.

Peace perhaps has never been experienced by the world. It is a narrow gulf, a gap been two wars. As long as two diverse principles exist in the universe, there can never be peace. Peace is only an ambition, a desire and a thought of those who do not understand the diverse ways of the two principles in life and the universe. The sages attained a state of nonattachment and wisdom and remained unaffected by the turbulences of life. There is no other way for peace but to go to the deep silence where She resides in Her majesty.

Joy lies in silence and stillness.

The Silence within the Sound

Hear the laughter
Mantra lives throughout
Thee in me
Me in Thee
Joy full.

Thy great gift of silence is worth more than
all the words man has spoken.

Formless Love,
Thy darkness holds all light,
Thy silence all sound.

I have no words today,
just quiet alertness.
Quite pleasurable.

Feeling Thy presence
All things become magical,
Wonder surrounds me.

Surrounded by noise,
one listens for the silence within the sound.

My Life

My life is a silence grasped by timeless hands;
The world is drowned in an immortal gaze.
Naked my spirit from its vestures stands;
I am alone with my own self for space.

I have seen the beauty of immortal eyes,
And heard the passion of the lover's flute,
And known a deathless ecstasy's surprise,
And sorrow in my heart forever mute.

My heart is a center of infinity,
My body is a dot in the soul's expanse.
A momentless immensity pure and bare,
I stretch to an eternal everywhere.

What I realize is that the life force is upon me to do what God wants and not what I want. No one will be able to rob this conviction of mine. Many times I have had the feeling that in all decisive matters I was no longer alone and was beyond time. I felt I was an ancient traveler and belonged to the centuries. Suddenly I would get stunned and go into silence.

Whenever I have sought human help, it did not work. Sometimes I have felt with all my profundity as though a breath of the infinite world of stars and endless space has touched me. When I bathe in sunlight with the winds and clouds moving over me, my experience becomes inexplicable.

Two Realities

I remember it precisely.
One evening in the stillness of the night I heard a
soundless voice saying—I am with you.
I listened, fascinated. It was late winter of late spring.

It was not unusual for me to tune into the chords of
nature.
In the background I could hear soft music containing
as well the discords of nature.
Nature is not always completely harmonious; she can
also be dreadfully contradictory.
The music was that way too: An outpouring of sound
having the quality of silent drizzling rain and
gushing wind.
It is simply impossible to describe it.

I gently opened my eyes and unbolted the shutters.
There was no one in sight.
And nothing to be heard, no wind, nothing,
nothing at all.

This is strange I thought. I was certain.
But apparently I had been daydreaming.
In the middle of this I fell asleep and at once the same
dream persisted.
At this point I woke up,
same still night with a still moonlight.

For me this dream represented the equivalent of reality
but in an unknown state.
That night everything seemed so real,
I could scarcely sort out the two realities.

Night

Night falls gently, the beautiful luminous night,
Pale green sky tender like a flower.
Someone playing flute notes is heard in the distance.

Grief is limited by the limits of our life.
I can die; I have nothing more to fear.

I feel the tender compassion of my love of loves
Floating in the air.

Light! Thou art so beautiful.
Now pour upon my brow
The long sleep that knows no dreams.

Oh, affectionate breath of the deep earth,
kiss me once again.
Let ever thy lips evaporate into the Silence.

CHAPTER SEVEN

THE ANSWER

And so now we can answer the question. The most ancient traveler in this universe is neither man nor woman, but a mystery without which our existence would become in vain. That mystery can not be unveiled by the intellect or intellectual pursuits, nor by psychological analysis or scientific experiments. That mystery is unveiled only to those fortunate few who learn to love others and make love the goal of life. It is the very basis of life on this planet.

Love is the most ancient traveler from aeons past,
Ever young and fresh it will for eternity last.

Blessed are those who are lost in the philosophy of love.

CHAPTER EIGHT

ADIEU

<u>Farewell</u>

I am an ancient traveler
on the path of the unknown.
I weave a garland to salute the night,
and fill the basket of farewell to night.

Nothingness

Like a candle
I am melting in his fire,
amidst the flames
out flashing.
I passed away into nothingness,
I vanished.

Soooooooooooooooooooo

A hummingbird flew up to my face
And looked at me eye to eye

Hummmmmmmmmmmm

Off

Swami Rama

Swami Rama was born in the Himalayas and was initiated by his master into many yogic practices. His master also sent him to other yogis and adepts of the Himalayas to gain new perspectives and insights into the ancient teachings. At the young age of 24 he was installed as Shankaracharya of Karvirpitham in South India. Swamiji relinquished this position to pursue intense sadhana in the caves of the Himalayas. Having successfully completed this sadhana, he was directed by his master to go to Japan and to the West in order to illustrate the scientific basis of the ancient yogic practices. At the Menninger Foundation in Topeka, Kansas, Swamiji convincingly demonstrated the capacity of the mind to control so-called involuntary physiological processes such as the heart rate, body temperature and brain waves. Swamiji's work in the United States continued for 23 years, and during this period he established the Himalayan International Institute.

Swamiji became well known in the United States as a yogi, teacher, philosopher, poet, humanist, and philanthropist. His models of preventive medicine, holistic health, and stress management have permeated the mainstream of Western medicine. In 1993 Swamiji returned to India where he established the Himalayan Institute Hospital Trust in the foothills of the Garhwal Himalayas. Swamiji left this physical plane in November, 1996, but the seeds he has sown continue to sprout, bloom, and bear fruit. His teachings, embodied in the words, "Love, Serve, Remember," continue to inspire the many students whose good fortune it has been to come into contact with such an accomplished, selfless and loving master.